LESSONS LEARNED

211 Years of Transforming Knowledge into Wisdom

SHAILENDRA THOMAS   DIANNA HATFIELD

BECKY CRAIG   RHIANNON THURMAN

LAURIE THAMES   SARA MALONE   TRISH BAKER

SHAYNE KASSELMAN   CORIENNE MULLINS

RACHEL MONTGOMERY

MLStimpson Enterprises

Published by Edifying Reads, MLStimpson Enterprises

P.O. Box 1592

Cedar Hill, TX 75106-1592

ISBN: 978-1-943563-22-7

Cover design by Jesse Skidmore

Editing by Trisha Heddlesten and Lisa Moreno

DEDICATION

This book is dedicated to all of the Christian Educators who inspire and prepare youth to be "salt and light" in an ever-changing world.
Matthew 5:13-16

CONTENTS

Acknowledgments   vii

Introduction   ix

1. Enough!   1

2. Perfect   5

3. What's in a Name?   11

4. The Best Day Ever   15

5. Bittersweet   19

6. Desire   23

7. Laughter   33

8. The Thanks We Get   37

9. Learning from My Students   41

10. Don't Believe Everything You Hear   45

11. Today Might be the Day   49

12. There's No "I" in Teach!   53

13. Handwriting WITH Tears   57

14. Amazing Grace   61

15. Lessons Learned   65

About the Authors   71

ACKNOWLEDGMENTS

We would like to express our sincere appreciation to Michelle Stimpson (publisher), Jesse Skidmore (cover concept & design), and Trisha Heddlesten & Lisa Moreno (editors). The completion of this book could not have been possible without their contributions, assistance and participation.

INTRODUCTION

Some of us have known since childhood that we wanted to teach, some of us decided in college, and some of us came to the teaching profession via an unforeseen career change, but all of us felt on that first day in the classroom that we were going to change the world, one student at a time. We felt that God had imparted to us the spiritual gift of teaching, and we wanted to pour all we had into those placed under our charge. We knew that we had knowledge, both from our college degrees and from life, and the students needed it. Little did we know that we would be the ones learning, daily.

We quickly came to the realization that possessing knowledge is one thing but knowing how to use it is quite another. Knowledge is what you know. Wisdom is knowing what to do with what you know. Through days, weeks, months, and years of working with students, we were able to gain divine insight and understanding (wisdom) that allowed us to love unconditionally, forgive, encourage, and disciple while living purposeful Christian lives professionally and personally.

Colossians 2:2-3 states, "My goal is that they may be encouraged in heart and united in love, so that they may have the full riches of complete understanding, in order that they may know the mystery of God, namely, Christ, in whom are hidden all the treasures of wisdom and knowledge." We discovered hidden treasures of wisdom and knowledge daily as we created and maintained a learning environment that inclined students' hearts toward Christ and provided a firm academic foundation.

Step into our classrooms and catch a glimpse of our 211 years of turning knowledge into wisdom. Take a peek into our Lessons Learned. Lessons that enlighten, encourage, uplift, inspire, motivate, and inform everyday living.

CHAPTER 1
ENOUGH!

E nough....it's a word that we never seem to have *enough* of. Do I have *enough* time to finish this lesson? Did I buy *enough* supplies for this project? Will I make *enough* money to support my family? Have my students learned *enough* to succeed? These are all questions that will come up throughout your teaching experience. I have found that the one that can cripple me if I let it is: AM I ENOUGH?

Teaching is a calling; there's no doubt about it. We are called to inform minds, build character, and foster spiritual growth. James 3:1 says, "Not many of you should become teachers, my fellow believers, because you know that we who teach will be judged more strictly." That is a solemn warning, but it also shows me what a powerful calling this is. Looking at my own skill set and abilities, it can seem daunting to call myself a teacher. Even after 17 years of teaching, I find myself facing situations that I haven't faced before. Each day brings new challenges. I can find myself asking that haunting question, "Am I *enough*?"

It may surprise you to know that the answer is, "NO!" We are all limited in our abilities and knowledge, but that's the beauty of it. We're not called to be enough. We're called to surrender. The Holy Spirit working within us enables us to fulfill this high calling of teaching. I Corinthians 1:26-31 has always been such a comfort and encouragement to me. "Brothers and sisters, think of what you were when you were called. Not many of you were wise by human standards; not many were influential; not many were of noble birth. But God chose the foolish things of the world to shame the wise; God chose the weak things of the world to shame the strong. God chose the lowly things of this world and the despised things—and the things that are not—to nullify the things that are, so that no one may boast before him. It is because of him that you are in Christ Jesus, who has become for us wisdom from God—that is, our righteousness, holiness and redemption. Therefore, as it is written: Let the one who boasts boast in the Lord."

My inability is the conduit for Christ's glory. I'm reminded of the old saying, "God doesn't call the qualified; He qualifies the called." His equipping in my life has prepared me more than anything else for teaching. It is so comforting to be able to pray and allow God to work in situations that I am not *enough* to handle on my own. There have been many situations where I can feel Him at work.

This equipping is not passive. There are certainly things I should be doing to help equip myself. Each year, I grow and learn as a teacher. I attend training, learn new techniques and strategies, collaborate with other teachers, develop a growth mindset, and consistently evaluate and look for areas of improvement. I'm never satisfied with the status quo. One of the beautiful things about God's equipping is that He always calls us to do our best.

Colossians 3:23 states, "Whatever you do, work at it with all your heart, as working for the Lord, not for human masters". I've discovered through my years of teaching, that if I do my part, and depend on the Lord to fulfill His calling in me, I AM ENOUGH.

E - "**Except** the LORD build the house, they labour in vain that build it: except the LORD keep the city, the watchman waketh but in vain." Psalm 127:1 (KJV)

N - "**Not** that we are competent in ourselves to claim anything for ourselves, but our competence comes from God."
II Corinthians 3:5

O - "**Oh**, fear the Lord, ye his saints: for there is no want to them that fear him." Psalm 34:9 (KJV)

U - "I **urge** you to live a life worthy of the calling you have received." Ephesians 4:1b

G - "My **grace** is sufficient for you, for my power is made perfect in weakness. Therefore I will boast all the more gladly about my weaknesses, so that Christ's power may rest on me."
II Corinthians 12:9

H - "And **He** gave some, apostles; and some, prophets; and some, evangelists; and some, pastors and teachers; For the perfecting of the saints, for the work of the ministry, for the edifying of the body of Christ." Ephesians 4:11-12

LESSON LEARNED

Jesus is Enough! I am enough because Jesus is enough, and Jesus lives in me.

The one who calls you is faithful, and he will do it. I Thessalonians 5:24

PERSONAL REFLECTION

_____

_____

_____

_____

_____

_____

_____

_____

_____

_____

_____

_____

_____

_____

_____

_____

_____

_____

_____

_____

_____

_____

_____

_____

_____

CHAPTER 2
PERFECT

C lassrooms are interesting places and often a glimpse into the community in which they are located. The majority of the students in my homeroom were students from middle class families, from a middle-class suburb, with all the trappings that a middle-class income could afford. Piano and violin lessons, soccer and baseball leagues, and summer vacays were all prerequisites. My students spent an average of 175 days a year completing class work, homework, and projects with the goal of moving on to the next grade.

My career was perfect. I had settled into a nice routine of open houses, instruction, tests, report cards, an occasional special program, and then summer break. It's amazing how fast the school years roll by. Before I could blink, my first year of teaching was over, then my second, then my fifth. It is hard to believe that I now find myself in my 10th year.

I was very satisfied with my routine until I met Jonathan. Jonathan was not like the community children. He was aloof – too aloof – almost like he wanted to disappear. He did not bring any school supplies and never returned homework. His previous teachers told me that he probably had a learning difference and needed to be tested for special education.

Jonathan would spend his recess alone looking at the grass or sky or playing with a small car. The other children seemed to ignore him. Did they even see him? They never spoke to him in a positive or negative manner. It was as though he did not exist.

During class discussions Jonathan was always quiet. He never volunteered to answer any questions. His work was subpar, to say it lightly, and I could barely read his writing. He was reading two years below level and could barely count. How was I supposed to teach a child like this? Surely, he could not be from this community. I half-heartedly tried to help him by offering 10- or 15-minute tutoring sessions during the day, but soon tired of spending my planning time helping him.

By Thanksgiving, I was weary of trying to reach out to Jonathan. I told the principal that I was going to complete the special education paperwork and submit it when we returned from Thanksgiving break. As I was completing the paperwork, I had an inclination to pray. I am embarrassed to say that I had not specifically prayed for Jonathan at all over the previous months.

As I was praying, I felt that I needed to wait. I put the special education paperwork away and argued with God for the rest of the day and all night. I felt that God was impressing on my spirit to work with this child. But I did have a few counter arguments. I did not have time to work with him, and I did not have a degree in special education. And the final argument - my career was perfect, and this situation disrupted my perfect situation. But by morning, I cried uncle, surrendered, and asked God to give me the wisdom to teach this child.

I sent a note home to his mother telling her that I was going to start working with him for 45 minutes after school, three times per week. I never received a response back from his mother, but Jonathan just started staying after school.

It was difficult to know what he knew or did not know, because he failed every test. I decided to start each lesson with a story about cars because I often saw him playing with a small car on the playground. To my surprise, he acted like he was interested in the car story. I asked a question about the color of the car, and he answered correctly. I asked what letter of the alphabet the word car began with and he gave another correct answer. I asked if he could find the word race on the page and got another correct response. So, I decided to go a step further. I taught him how to sound out some words and asked him to read those words in a sentence. To my astonishment, after a couple of attempts, he was able to decode the words and read the sentence. I jumped up and down. I shouted. I praised him. (Happy Dance!) Did I see a little smile on his face? This was the first smile I had seen all year long.

Over the next several months of tutoring, I reviewed every foundational literacy skill I knew. After a few weeks, I noticed how fast he was catching on and improving. He was also performing better in class and answering a few questions. I could tell he was feeling more comfortable in my classroom.

Jonathan was doing so well, I decided I wanted to reach out to his mother. After several attempts, his mother finally came to the school. We were able to visit, and I discovered that she was a very young single mother who had not graduated high school, was working as a waitress, and was struggling just to keep food on the table. But, of course, she still wanted but the best for her young son. I was able to connect her to my church for some much-needed support.

I finally spoke to the class about how our society is made up of all different types of individuals and that we should be kind to everyone because all were created in the image of God. Reluctantly, the other students started to play with Jonathan. Soon, they got to know and like him and began including him in classroom games.

By the end of the school year, Jonathan was almost on grade level and had made great strides academically and socially. I know most would say that I really helped Jonathan. But the truth is that Jonathan really helped me. He changed my perspective on teaching. I was a teacher that only taught students who already knew how to learn, students who could have really taught themselves. I had to dig deep professionally and spiritually to teach Jonathan and truly trust God to give me and Jonathan what we needed to succeed in the classroom. Through Jonathan, I was able to see the life-changing power of God in the life of a young child and his mother. My career was perfect, again.

The last time I heard about Jonathan, he was a high school senior making A's and B's, with many friends, and college bound. I still regularly pray for Jonathan and thank God for bringing that young man into my life.

LESSON LEARNED
Never give up. His Grace is sufficient. The challenges are where the real work is.
But He said to me, "My Grace is sufficient for you, for my power is made perfect in weakness." 2 Corinthians 12:9a

PERSONAL REFLECTION

CHAPTER 3
WHAT'S IN A NAME?

The room was ready, everything was in its place, the goodies were waiting on each child's desk. It was the beginning of the school year, and as a teacher, I had spent days getting everything ready for this new group of children. I had looked at the roster that was given to me. Names, names . . . all kinds of names were staring at me from the paper. I knew a couple of them as the younger sibling of a child I had taught in the years before, but many were new names. I had already been praying for this group that would be with me for the coming year.

The door opened, and several came in and began finding their desks on this orientation day. They began to unpack the supplies that they had brought. There was good interaction between me and the parents and the students' little faces were both tentative and excited for a new school year. As I greeted each one, I wondered what each one would be like in the upcoming year.

As I was contemplating this, the door opened and in ran a

blond-headed, happy little boy. He ran right up to greet me. I said "Hi! And what is your name?" He answered right away, "Sammy No!" I said, "Well, nice to meet you Sammy!" He began looking for his desk. I, in the meantime began looking at my list looking for Sammy and how his last name was spelled. I could not find it. Just then a mom, who I assumed was his mother following him, walked through my classroom door. I went to introduce myself to her and she said she was Mrs. Smith. I knew I had no "Smith" on my list. She went on to say, "I see that Sammy made it in here already!"

At this point I was confused and said that he had come in and told me his name was "Sammy No." Now the mother looked confused. Then I saw on her face a look of understanding, then she chuckled and looked a bit sheepish. She said, "I am so sorry, this is on me, I think we say at home 'Sammy, no!' so often that he thinks that is his last name!"

Later that evening, I was reflecting on this encounter, and a poignant thought came to me - It is so very important to KNOW each of these little ones entrusted to us and come to know, love, and pray for them as the unique individuals that the Lord made them to be.

Just as little Sammy was under the impression that he was a "Sammy No" instead of a "Sammy Smith," we sometimes misunderstand who we really are in Christ. We need to know our unique identity and hold onto the blessing each of us has in being fully and completely KNOWN by the Lord. Luke 12:7-8 tells us, "Indeed the very hairs of your head are all numbered. Don't be afraid. You are worth more than many sparrows." In Isaiah 49:16a, we see that God values each of us so much that He tells us, "See, I have engraved you on the palms of my hands..."

With every new school year, I am reminded that God loves

each of us so much that He wants to KNOW each of us completely – so much that He counts the hairs on our head and writes us on the palm of His hand. That is deep love.

As we teach these little ones each year, we can never love them as well as God does, but we can love and value each of them through God, teaching them about Him. They will know of His love through us. We can know that in the midst of life, with all its ups and downs, that the Lord loves each of us in the same deep way. We are valued and loved deeply by the Lord and can, in turn, love and give value to each of the little ones in our classes each year!

LESSON LEARNED

We each have a unique identity in Christ and are known completely by Him. We should strive to know each other as those loved deeply by God.

No, in all these things we are more than conquerors through him who loved us. For I am sure that neither death nor life, nor angels nor rulers, nor things present nor things to come, nor powers, nor height nor depth, nor anything else in all creation, will be able to separate us from the love of God in Christ Jesus our Lord.

Romans 8:37-39

Personal Reflection

_____
_____
_____
_____
_____
_____
_____

CHAPTER 4
THE BEST DAY EVER

As a veteran lower elementary teacher of three decades, I've had many busy days and I've had days that have just seemed to drag. Most days go according to my lesson plans and I'm very efficient in getting through my objectives in a timely manner. But there is nothing better than telling your students that it's time to pack up and they say, "What? It seems like we just got here. This was the best day ever!"

Not only does this make me smile, it gives me positive feedback that we did, indeed, have a great day. It might be because we played a fun game, did a special writing project, had a fun craft, or just had a normal day. I know that it means I did a good job teaching in an upbeat, fun manner. That hopefully I reached all the students at the level where they are. That no matter how challenging, or perhaps boring, the information I presented that day was, it was still well received.

On the flip side, this makes me think about what happens when a day doesn't go so well. Perhaps there were multiple interruptions, behavior issues, or conflicts with another classmate that had to be dealt with, a lesson just didn't flow the way I thought it should, or maybe I was grumpy and short on patience. As a teacher, I am always cognizant of the days, weeks, and months as the school year progresses, because we must master a certain amount of instructional material by year end. But I also must be flexible and willing to try other methods of reaching my students as needed.

Teaching is a hard, challenging, and exhausting profession. But having days when your students say that this was the "best day ever", makes me pause and appreciate my class. I'm not teaching mini-adults, I'm teaching young children. I need to enjoy their enthusiasm, smiles, and laughter. Yes, they may make corny jokes and tell me riddles and knock- knock jokes that force me to put on a fake smile. They're children! I need to always remember that I'm teaching someone's precious baby whom they love more than anything. While it's important to keep our standards high, it's just as important to make a connection with each child who comes into your classroom. I need to try to see life through the eyes of a child, not a jaded adult. Often, their prayers teach me to pray with child-like faith, knowing that God is listening. I need to get excited and clap my hands, as my students do when I tell them a story from the Bible. I need to enjoy each day as a gift from God.

LESSON LEARNED

Every day can be the best day ever if you delight in your work,
knowing it is God's work.
*Whatever you do, work at it with all your heart, as working for the Lord,
not for men.* Colossians 3:23

PERSONAL REFLECTION

_____

_____

_____

_____

_____

_____

_____

_____

_____

_____

_____

_____

_____

_____

_____

_____

_____

_____

_____

_____

_____

_____

_____

CHAPTER 5
BITTERSWEET

I've just finished another year of teaching. I've been in the classroom for three decades, which is amazing for someone who wanted to be a stay at home mom and possibly homeschool my children. I wanted to live in the country on some land. In reality, I didn't home school, and we live in the urban sprawl of Dallas! In life, we need to plan, but then let God be in control. I remind myself of this as I brace myself for the ending of another school year.

As I woke up on the last day of school this year, my first thought was one of relief. Hooray, I made it through another year! And then I thought of my sweet class and how I would miss them. I was flooded with bittersweet feelings. The definition of bittersweet is "sweet with a bitter aftertaste." I think that is an accurate description of how I feel at the end of every school year: both happy and sad. We are all in need of a break, but I also know that "my kids" won't be my kids next year. I must let them go.

This makes me think of life in general. I just had my 60th

birthday, and it was shocking to me that I had turned 20 three times! I think all of life is bittersweet. It's wonderful to see your child sit up, crawl, and then learn to walk. But it seems like you turn around and they're graduating high school, off to college, then finding a career, moving to another state, or even overseas! Bittersweet! You are enjoying life in the town or city you're living in, serving in your church, and then God calls you to another location. Bittersweet!

You enjoy sweet times of fellowship with friends and then one day you get that phone call. There's been an accident or a terminal diagnosis, and life changes. A marriage is in crisis and perhaps ends in divorce. There is a downsizing at work and suddenly you're not needed anymore, and you get to experience the world of unemployment. These situations are mostly bitter, but if we are willing to look for it, there is usually a sweet nugget of truth that God is trying to teach us in the mist of these unfortunate circumstances. Bittersweet!

Your precious child into whom you've poured your life makes bad choices. These are choices that mom and dad can't change, but the child is learning and maturing through the process of dealing with the consequences. Bittersweet!

My relationship with my Lord and Savior has highs and lows. Sometimes I feel like I am successfully following Christ, and then a trial comes, and I start fretting and worrying. What happened to my faith? What happened to listening to the same godly counsel I've given to others? Bittersweet!

I enjoy bittersweet chocolate because the bitter flavor is just enough to make the sweetness richer. If I want to enjoy the sweet moments in my life, I'll have to take the bitter that goes along with it. I'm thankful that I can always trust God and that He is always "sweet" towards me even during bitter circumstances. The scriptures often speak of the goodness of God. I can't see His grand plan, but I have decided to trust and believe that God is always good. He is not bittersweet, but faithful and good, through and through. Amen!

LESSON LEARNED
We must accept both the bitter and sweet moments in life to experience God's goodness.

Taste and see that the Lord is good, blessed is the one who takes refuge in Him.
Psalm 34:8

Personal Reflection

_____

_____

_____

_____

_____

_____

_____

_____

_____

_____

_____

_____

_____

_____

_____

_____

_____

_____

CHAPTER 6
DESIRE

We all have desires. Our desires direct where we spend our time and the quality with which we do an activity. What does desire have to do with obtaining an education? How does the desire to learn, the desire to teach, and the desire to parent affect the education process?

Desire to Learn

My first year of teaching was in a city that had a very high illiteracy and teenage pregnancy rate. I taught in a large high school that had one principal and six vice principals. Outside of the school was a large grassy area with a fence surrounding almost the entire property. There was an unspoken rule, known throughout the school, that any student trying to leave school grounds to ditch class had to reach this fence before one of the six vice principals – each physically fit and agile – caught up and dragged him or her back into class. When attendance was taken each period, any students missing from class were hunted for in the hallways and bathrooms. If they couldn't be located there, the race to the fence was on between the students and vice principal. If a student could get up and over the fence before the vice-principal nabbed him, the vice principal would not go beyond the fence to bring him back. However, if the vice principal caught him, he was coming back to class. Personally, I didn't want that student back in my class. If he wanted to be gone that badly, then let him be gone!

I taught full-time at this school for several months before I was asked to also teach some night school classes at the same school. I agreed and was amazed at the difference I saw between the students who attended school during normal school hours and those who attended at night. It was a night and day difference literally and figuratively! The students who attended night school had full- or part-time jobs during the day. Many were teen moms and dads. The realities of life were upon these students, and they were motivated to finish their high school education. They could see the benefits of having an education, and they worked hard at it. Their desire was evident as they worked hard, finished their homework, and asked questions in class. They wanted to learn.

The students who attended school during the day were a typical mixture of some motivated and interested students, students who had no desire whatsoever to be there, and everything in between. As a first-year teacher, I was amazed at the difference I witnessed in these two groups of students, and I began to see, from a teacher's perspective, the impact that student desire had on a student gaining a quality education.

The heart of the discerning acquires knowledge, for the ears of the wise seek it out. Proverbs 18:15

ONE STUDENT WHOM I ADMIRE THAT EXEMPLIFIED THIS concept is Garrett. Garrett struggled in school, but he worked diligently each day to stay on top of his assignments. He asked questions in class. He let me know when I was going too fast for him. The other students would become impatient as he wrote each word carefully during a spelling test or copied my notes from the front screen. He was an active kid and enjoyed doing most anything outdoors, but he even asked to come in at recess at times for help on assignments that he was struggling with. Garrett had a desire to learn. Gaining an education was valuable to him; it didn't come easy to him, but he worked hard anyhow. His desire influenced my desire to teach him. I did not mind taking my break at recess to work with him nor did I mind going slower on material so that he could take in what he needed at the speed that he could process it. I was confident that Garrett was doing all that he could and working to his ability level as he earned As and Bs, with an occasional C. His grades would have been much lower without his work ethic and desire to learn.

Seeking knowledge requires action. The seeking part shows desire. The seeker wants something...knowledge. Garrett wants knowledge. He doesn't allow his learning challenges to stop him from gaining an education. He pursues it with all that he can.

Since that first experience, I have taught for many years in several states across the country, in both public schools and private Christian schools. I have taught a wide range of ages and subject areas, and the school sizes have ranged from quite small to average to quite large. I have encountered students who struggle to learn most any subject, students who excel in some subjects but struggle in others, and students who seem to grasp on-level material very quickly no matter what the subject is. But one factor is constant: a desire to learn significantly improves a student's performance in the classroom.

Desire to Teach

I know my desire to teach is strong, because it had to weather quite the storm and has survived. After my first teaching experience in Georgia, I was wiped out! I was a first-year teacher and away from friends and family or any type of support system. I did not have my own classroom. Instead, I had a cart I pushed from room to room and taught in other teachers' classrooms when they had a planning period. Those teachers usually exited their classrooms to give me my own space to teach, but not always. My students would file in while I set up. Then I tore everything down and packed up at the end of each class to move on to my next class. If students wanted to find me for extra help before or after school, I shared a large office area with five other teachers. So, any of our students had to come find us there and be willing to ask questions surrounded by the noise of other students asking questions. Typically, the first year of teaching is tough, but these conditions added to the brutality, and I decided that I had had enough of teaching.

I left the state of Georgia and headed back to the familiar grounds of Nebraska where I had friends and family. I was newly engaged and ready to start a new life and some other type of career. I applied for a job at a museum where I would run exhibits and direct museum events. I was called in for an interview and was offered the job. As I prayed about taking it, I didn't sense the Lord's leading in it at all. I turned it down because it really was too far for me to drive, the hours seemed too long, and the pay was not great. Soon after turning that job down, I saw a job for a teaching position at a Christian high school. The desire in me was reignited, and I decided to try teaching again. I applied and was offered the job. The distance to the school was just as far as it was to the museum; the hours were longer, and the pay was worse, but this time God was in it.

He placed a desire in me to be back in the classroom and influencing lives for Him. Any time over the last twenty years when I have taken a break in my teaching career to have kids, be a stay-at-home mom, etc., I have still been a tutor or taught Sunday school at church. God has drawn me back into teaching time and time again, and not extinguished that drive and desire to be an influencer on others' lives.

In the numerous schools in which I have taught, I have rubbed shoulders with many, many teachers. Most are true teachers at heart. They work hard. They think up creative ways to teach their students - about how to challenge the accelerated student, how to encourage the student who has given up, and how to meaningfully reach the overlooked student. They try new techniques even when they've been teaching for years. They pray faithfully for their students and families. I think of these teachers as "the mighty thirty."

In II Samuel 23 and I Chronicles 11, a list of names is recorded of around thirty men who were David's greatest support. I Chronicles 11:10 states, "These were the chiefs of David's mighty warriors - they, together with all Israel, gave his kingship strong support to extend it over the whole land, as the Lord had promised." I could easily list thirty mighty teachers with whom I have had the privilege of teaching: the consistent and faithful Kindergarten teacher who stays well past her official hours, the fun and bubbly Art teacher who thinks of each student as she decides which art piece each one should design, the pre-K teacher who pleasantly instructs her students on restroom etiquette and hallway manners, the high school teacher who refuses to let Bible class be boring but enlivens the class with his thought-provoking questions, the 5th grade teacher who listens intently to her students and makes each one feel personally cared for. The list could continue for several pages. God has placed a desire in them to teach despite poor pay, critical parents, and uncooperative students. They give their all, and they come to the aid of others around them who are having a rough day. I have benefitted many times from these teachers personally. They are truly "mighty in the LORD."

I have also met some teachers whose desire to teach is gone. Maybe it was never there to begin with. Teaching is drudgery to them. Their complaints far outweigh their delights in the classroom. No amount of small success achieved by a student is noticed. They do whatever they can to not be in their classrooms doing their job because they don't desire to do it. It goes without saying that these teachers do not bring out the best in their students, and their students' education is no doubt compromised because of the teacher's lack of desire.

Desire to Parent

Parents come in all varieties, as do students and teachers. Some are very involved in their child's education, some are unaware of their responsibilities, and the rest fall somewhere in between.

"Because the Lord disciplines those he loves,
as a father the son he delights in."
Proverbs 3:12

I am a parent myself and see education from both perspectives (as parent and teacher). Sometimes I go into "teacher mode," at home and sometimes I change into "parent mode" at school. I fully understand that in both worlds I'm occasionally running completely on "survival mode." However, the ideal is that I delight in whatever task the Lord has set before me and that I take on each responsibility with His help, His love, His desire, and His strength. Education is a partnership. For it to run at its ideal state, the student, teacher, and parent each have responsibilities and parts that significantly affect the others.

Most students are not born with the innate ability to plan and organize. These skills are taught, at home and at school. The parents who desire a high-quality education for their children will take the time and effort that is necessary to help their children experience academic success.

Unfortunately, some parents do not demonstrate the desire to support their children. They take a very hands-off approach. If a student's grades are failing, they do not offer help at home nor do they make any changes at home to improve their child's performance.

Some parents are facing challenges that make it very difficult to even provide for and care for their children, among their other responsibilities, let alone stay actively involved in their children's schooling. These parents might feel grieved that they can't fulfill their desire to help their children excel in school.

Some parents don't understand the importance of instilling good work ethics and skills into their children that they will need for the rest of their lives. I have been fortunate enough to work with many parents who are advocates for their children. Advocating means helping the child understand what will be required of him to be successful in life. Those requirements may include extra time spent on homework, studying for tests/quizzes well in advance, spending time on Saturdays working on long-term projects, etc. Advocating for a child does not mean standing in the way of consequences falling on the child. Sometimes I hear the panic in a parent's voice at progress report time when a failing grade is noticed. If the grade reaches a passing level at the lowest possible point level, the panic subsides.

My hope for these families is that they would focus on the child throughout the year to observe if he has mastered the material in that particular subject. Is he prepared to move on to the next learning objective or subject that would build on this current knowledge? In my experience, the grade is not as important as mastering the skills, concepts, and knowledge necessary.

So, how does desire affect the education process? We can see from the above examples that the desires of students, teachers, and parents all affect the education process. When desire for an education is high, it has a positive impact on the others. If one part of the triad displays low aspirations, the whole process may come to a standstill. We can help each other through the doldrums that hit us on the path of gaining an education. The ultimate reward is the education itself and the career and skills we acquire because of the education.

Remember the long-term goal - to equip students academically and spiritually. Set up rewards to motivate and celebrate successes together. Turn to others for support and be a support for others when they are floundering. All three parties (students, teachers, and parents) are important and significant. We're a team. Don't micromanage and take over a part that is not yours to take. Allow parents do their jobs. Allow students do their jobs. Allow teachers to do their jobs. Ask for help and support as needed. Conference as an entire group to build rapport and keep lines of communication open. Progress will breed desire, and desire for a high-quality education will ultimately bring success.

LESSON LEARNED

Desire matters. God will place a desire in your heart for the work
He has equipped you to do.
Take delight in the Lord, and he will give you the desires of your heart.
Psalm 37:4

PERSONAL REFLECTION

_____
_____
_____
_____
_____
_____
_____
_____
_____
_____
_____
_____
_____
_____
_____
_____
_____
_____

CHAPTER 7
LAUGHTER

I love to laugh! It relieves stress, and according to Proverbs 17:22, it is good medicine. You also use more facial muscles when you frown rather than smile. Have you ever tried to frown while laughing? There is something infectious about a good belly laugh with a friend, student, or colleague. There are times we end up laughing so much it hurts.

There is so much turmoil in this world. I don't even like to listen to the news anymore. I used to be an avid reader of the Dallas Morning News. For years, I faithfully read it daily. Now there's not a lot to laugh about when you hear the news, but we still get to choose our response to troubling headlines.

Every day in the classroom, teachers are faced with many difficult situations. It's easy to lose patience with a student over a discipline issue or academic matter. We all have a choice to make when faced with a trying circumstance. We can choose annoyance, impatience, frustration, or crying and make ourselves more miserable. Or we can choose to take a deep breath, maybe count to ten, and then show patience and a cheerful smile, perhaps turning the incident into a laugh.

At a staff Christmas party one year, we were asked to answer the question "If you could give one thing to your fellow teachers, what would it be?" As I waited for my turn and thought about what I would say, it came quite easily to me. I would give everyone a good laugh every day. I'm not talking about laughing at someone else's expense of course, that's being unkind.

I often find myself doing something very silly in class because I was in a hurry and wasn't thinking things through. Rather than getting upset, I choose to laugh. My students see me laughing at some mistake I have made and hopefully they learn that it's okay to make mistakes.

We study the life of Helen Keller each year in my classroom and I love her story. Towards the end of the book, I always ask my students, "Which disability would you choose, being blind or deaf?". This leads to a great discussion. I always answer that I would rather be deaf than blind because I would feel so helpless if I was blind. I like to think that I'm capable and independent. But when Helen Keller answered this question in an interview, she responded that she would choose to be blind. She mentioned that she could use her senses to imagine what things looked like in her brain but that she would have a hard time imagining what music sounded like or someone's voice. Personally, I would miss the sound of laughter.

I enjoy praying and consider it a privilege when others seek me out to pray for a specific request. I try to write it down so that I don't forget.. Then I try to follow up with them and ask about their prayer request. When it's appropriate, I try to put a smile on their face by encouraging them. Life is full of trials that we must take seriously. That's why the gift of laughter is so important.

I have a square magnet on my refrigerator door that looks like a stone. There is one word printed one that magnet: LAUGH. I think that's a good reminder for all of us. Choose to laugh daily.

LESSON LEARNED

A positive outlook is as important as wisdom when it comes to handling difficult situations. We can each choose joy in every circumstance.

Rejoice in the Lord always. I will say it again: Rejoice!
Philippians 4:4

Personal Reflection

_____

_____

_____

_____

_____

_____

_____

_____

_____

_____

_____

_____

_____

_____

_____

_____

_____

_____

CHAPTER 8
THE THANKS WE GET

re you familiar with a song from the 90s titled "Thank You" by the Christian music artist Ray Boltz? Talk about a powerful song! It is about the blessings we will receive one day in heaven from those we have influenced for God. We might have encouraged someone in their walk with Jesus or led someone to accept Christ as their personal Savior. Because we have chosen the pathway of teaching, maybe even at a Christian school, that song has another level of significance. Its message holds the possibility that we can be a blessing to others for Christ in our teaching.

As teachers, we have a platform to teach not just the subject matter, but as Christ-followers, we can influence and lead students to Christ while making an impact on the future of our country and the world! It is a great , and sometimes scary responsibility, to realize that God wants us to represent His Kingdom every day in the classroom! One way we can do this is to plant seeds of righteousness in our relationships with students and colleagues.

Our lives should reflect the holiness of God by our actions, speech and character. The Bible states in Proverbs 11:18b, that the one who sows righteousness reaps a sure reward.

Another way is to see our role of teacher as one of honor and privilege. As a child of God, it is to serve Him in our profession! One way you can honor Him is by caring and loving others. John 13:34-35 says, "Love one another. . . By this everyone will know that you are my disciples." He has given you unique gifts and circles of people that no one else can influence like you can! Whether you are just beginning your teaching journey, are midstream, or close to the end, you are influencing students for generations to come. WOW! That is a quite a calling!

Part of being a dedicated teacher is the time-consuming prep and paperwork, plus always "bringing your A-game" is stressful and draining . Despite these challenges, teacher want to *know* their students and help them recognize and mature the gifts that God has placed in them. Often students are unaware of gifts that they already possess, but we have the unique privilege of helping them realize those gifts.

One of the many benefits of hard work is that often God gives us blessings on this side of heaven. It may come in the form of seeing "learning light bulbs" turn on for a child, creating hope and understanding for a student, or watching their self-esteem rise with the success of a lesson learned that might have included a corrected mistake!

Teachers are very fortunate because we regularly get to receive those "thank yous," like the Ray Boltz song describes. This might come in the form of a parent, grandparent, or even a former student coming back to visit. What a thrill it is to hear about their success and the impact you had on their life!

Remember, "Let your light shine... and glorify your Father in heaven." (Matt.6:16) You have been called to an honorable profession and can use your God-given gifts as a teacher to inspire future generations!

LESSON LEARNED

Sometimes we are fortunate to receive actual thanks when giving our best, but even if we don't, we know our actions do not go unnoticed by God when we follow His leading.

God is not unjust; he will not forget your work and the love you have shown Him as you have helped his people and continue to help them.

Hebrews 6:10

PERSONAL REFLECTION

_____
_____
_____
_____
_____
_____
_____
_____
_____
_____
_____
_____
_____
_____
_____
_____

CHAPTER 9
LEARNING FROM MY STUDENTS

W hen I began teaching about 25 years ago, my thought was, "I can't wait for the students to learn from me." What I have discovered over the years is that it is I who have learned from my students. The main lessons that I have learned as a teacher are: it is important to be teachable, life is about second chances, and that God is the abundant giver of wisdom.

My students have taught me that being a teachable teacher is an essential ingredient for enjoying a harmonious student-teacher relationship during a 175 day school year. One of my biggest lessons on being teachable came when I taught PE, and a student asked if she could teach the PE class a game that she had invented. At first, I was reluctant to comply because I needed to complete a sports unit as a curriculum requirement. As I recalled the excitement that the student expressed when she showed me the neatly written game rules, the map, and materials required, I decided to allow the student to teach her game to the class on a

Friday afternoon. I decided that I would step back and fully enable the student to teach and lead the game during the class period. As I observed the student's joy while her classmates enthusiastically participated in the detailed game, I reflected on the ingenuity of my "game inventor" student, and the initiative she demonstrated to develop a well-thought-out activity for her classmates. I learned that I did not always have to be the "all-wise dispenser of knowledge," and that my students are capable of sharing their ingenious ideas with me, as well.

The second lesson I have gleaned from teaching is that everyone should give, and be given, a second chance. When I taught high school in a small town in Oklahoma, there was a student on my class roster who was known to display difficult behavior in class. I started to form a preconceived perspective about this student, which began to build an invisible wall between us. I began to feel the Lord reminding me that He is a God of second chances. If God could forgive me of anything, why couldn't I give this student a "clean slate" on which to start our school year? The Lord continued to dismantle the defense system that I had constructed and allowed me to build a "second chance" bridge, even though I had not had any interaction with the student previously. I asked the Lord to help me develop a professional and compassionate relationship with this student, and to have a godly rapport with this incoming student, and the rest of my classes. Because I did not place this student at a disadvantage based on his previous reputation, I believe our school year was more productive and learning was enhanced.

The final lesson that I have learned on the journey of teaching is that God is the gracious giver of all wisdom when I lack it (James 1:5). Years ago, I taught a student who had consistent behavioral struggles every single day of the first quarter of the school year. I was at my wit's end and did not know how to make a "breakthrough" with this student. When all else failed, I prayed. I felt the Lord directing me to talk briefly with the student, and just check in with them to see how things were going in her life.

Through God's leading, I noticed an opportunity for the student and I to talk for about ten minutes between classes. During the conversation, the student disclosed that she was not sleeping well because of worry, and that she did not know how to tell her parents. We talked through how to let her parents know. Through this situation and my obedience to Holy Spirit's direction, we were able to bring this situation to her parents attention. In this "divine appointment," God gave me the words to say, the ears to listen, and His divine wisdom in a situation where I lacked the wisdom.

Teaching is such a privilege, and it is all possible because of God's graciousness to me. I'm grateful to be used as a conduit of His love for my students. The all-wise, patient, and loving God is my master teacher, and I'm grateful to be serving Him in this profession.

LESSON LEARNED

It is important to be teachable, even if you are the teacher.
Get wisdom, get understanding; do not forget my words or turn away from them. Proverbs 4:5

Personal Reflection

_____

_____

_____

_____

CHAPTER 10
DON'T BELIEVE EVERYTHING YOU HEAR

M eet the Teacher night is usually one of my favorite events of the school year. If you know me, this should not come as a surprise, because I genuinely love talking to anyone and everyone I meet. This past year, however, was different because I shared this story with the incoming parents:

Two years ago, I had a precious little firecracker named Katie in my class. She was very dramatic and kept me on my toes even though she was only three. I lovingly joked that she was in fact a Three-nager (Noun: a person aged 3 years old, possessing the attitude and demeanor of a teenager). As a preschool teacher, I am on my feet all day and need to be able to move quickly. For this reason, I love ballet flats. Why not? They are budget friendly and come in every color and style imaginable! However, this is Texas and it gets HOT, so your feet will get sweaty. I would never commit a fashion faux pas by wearing socks and flats!!

So, I started sprinkling baby powder in my shoes every

morning before school. This worked wonders! My feet weren't sticky and the fashion police weren't alerted. The only down side to my beloved ballet flats are the wood chips on the playground. I am constantly slipping off my shoe to dump the wood chips out and exposing my white powdery feet. I never thought anyone noticed, but if you have been around young kids, you know they focus on things that can incriminate you, then they save this information for later use.

By my estimation, we were settling into the school year nicely. We even had our first outside-of-school social with parents and kiddos at a local park. This is when Katie's mom and I attempted to have our first "real" conversation. We talked in spurts for about two or three minutes amid constant interruptions by children needing help or wanting us to watch their antics. I don't know if you've ever tried to have an intelligent conversation with more than one three year old present, but it takes great patience and determination. I could see Katie's mom had something on her mind that she wanted to discuss. However, the circumstances and time did not allow us to continue. It was clearly past everyone's nap time, as indicated by the crying and melt-downs happening all around. Every mom in the park was trying desperately to save face and make an exit without causing any more of a scene.

I had no idea what Katie's mom wanted to talk about in the park, but I was sure it must be related to Katie's academic or spiritual growth at school. How wrong was I! After carpool one day, we were chatting outside my classroom when she looked at me with a rather embarrassed look on her face and said, "I need to talk to you about what Katie is saying about you." Gulp.! What could this possibly be about? I braced myself as her mom tried to downplay what she was saying by adding "I'm sure she is confused, she's 3." Katie mom continue on and stated that Katie was reporting quite emphatically that "Mrs. Thurman has yucky feet." Apparently, my "yucky" feet were the topic of conversation at their house every single night.

As I stood there listening to her say these strange things right to my face, you might wonder how you would handle this situation if you were in my shoes. Please remember, I teach preschool and I am very good at keeping my composure in the classroom. I pride myself on my patience and my ability to remain calm when the children are upset. But in this situation, I forgot all about that. Before I fully realized what I was doing, my shoe was off, powder was flying everywhere, and I was holding the shoe up to her face while frantically trying to defend myself. I remember insisting over and over I don't have yucky feet, look, look, see! They smell like baby powder!

I was so intent on defending my hygiene that I forgot parents and teachers were still walking in the hall and seeing this rather odd exchange. Once I was convinced she fully understood that I didn't have yucky feet, I calmed down and put my shoe back on. Katie's mom just smiled, grabbed Katie and walked away giggling.

Not my finest moment, obviously! For all you parents out there reading this, just know that your sweet precious children don't just tell you about us teachers, they also tell us about you! They are equal opportunity offenders. So, let's call a truce and the next time our eyes meet in carpool or walking in the hall and you think you know something unflattering, just remember, "Don't believe everything they say about me, and I won't believe everything they say about you!"

LESSON LEARNED

Misunderstandings happen, but if we approach each other with an attitude of openness and humor, we can find connection and laughter together.

A cheerful heart is good medicine, but a crushed spirit dries up the bones.

Proverbs 17:22

PERSONAL REFLECTION

_____

_____

_____

_____

_____

_____

_____

_____

_____

_____

_____

_____

_____

_____

_____

_____

_____

_____

_____

_____

_____

_____

_____

CHAPTER 11
TODAY MIGHT BE THE DAY

W alking into a classroom full of expectant faces and excited bodies can be both an exhilarating and frightening experience. Will all of my studying and preparation pay off? Will I be able to apply the methods and procedures to real life? Will I be able to answer every question, challenge every student, and impress every parent?

No. The reality is that my classroom is not a perfect world. There will be ups and downs, mistakes and successes, laughter and tears, from both the students and myself! The encouraging thing about teaching is that I am never left to my own devices. Just as I allow the students to encourage and challenge each other, I allow the Lord and my colleagues to encourage and challenge me.

There are days when I feel completely prepared – the day is going to be wonderful, all of the kids will get along, the lessons will be taught and applied. These are the reasons I became a teacher! But unexpectedly, one student is unkind to another, the classroom routine is changed, a colleague needs me to step in and help with her class...suddenly the perfect day has gone downhill. How am I going to choose to respond to these bumps in the road? I can let them completely ruin the day. I can let the negative thoughts regarding my teaching capability take over. I can come down on the students and "just get through" the day. It all boils down to a choice. I can choose to be rigid or I can choose to be flexible. I can choose to get angry because my perfect day is ruined, or I can choose to get creative and see how I can make it work. I can choose to remember why I am teaching at a Christian school.

Teaching at a Christian school gives me the great privilege of weaving God and His love for us into everything I say and do; however, this is also a great responsibility! Each morning, before the students enter the room, I must to put on the mindset of "today might be the day." The question is, the day for what? It might be the day those two students are kind to each other. Or the day the quiet student makes friends on the playground. Perhaps it will be the day that concept in math is finally grasped and I see light bulbs going off in the class. Maybe it will be the day the student with an academic challenge overcomes a huge obstacle and gains confidence. But, ultimately, today might be the day the love of God is understood and the decision to start a relationship with Him is made through Christ. This is the desire of my heart each day as those eager, young faces enter the classroom.

The Holy Spirit can work through unexpected people and situations to bring about His plan for His children. There is no greater privilege for a teacher, or anyone, than to be used by God to lead others to Him. That is why I start each day with prayer; why I spend more time on Bible lessons than anything else; why I let the children see how Jesus loves them; and why I try to point them to the Bible in every situation. The desire of my heart is for this day to be the day of their salvation.

An exciting aspect of teaching children is that what you teach and how you treat each child is being observed by many families. There have been times when it seemed I was teaching the student and the parents! Many parents are seeking help on how to train and guide their child. The fact they enrolled their child in a Christian school, thus making an investment in their child, signifies their desire to establish a strong foundation of Biblical values. This gives me a window of opportunity to speak into the lives of the whole family. Not every family will respond favorably, but, like the seeds sown in the four soils, some will take root and flourish, and some will not. My responsibility is to be the sower of God's love and truth; His promise is that His word will not come back empty, or void.

So, as I walk into my classroom, and my daily life, I can tell myself with great anticipation, today might be the day!

LESSON LEARNED

Each day is a new opportunity to speak truth to someone, and you never know what fruit will come from planting seeds and allowing God to work through you.

Others, like seed sown on good soil, hear the Word, accept it, and produce a crop - some thirty, some sixty, some a hundred times what was sown.

Mark 4:20

Personal Reflection

_____

_____

_____

_____

CHAPTER 12

THERE'S NO "I" IN TEACH!

he Israelites were facing abysmal odds as they squared off against the Amalekite army (Exodus 17:8-13). Their leader, Moses, knew something had to be done. He sent Joshua and the army to fight the Amalekites while he went to the top of the hill with the staff of God. Moses lifted the staff to Heaven as a picture of their dependence on God. When he did this, the Israelites prevailed in the battle. The only problem was, Moses got tired. His arms began to ache, and his knees became weak. He was only human, and although he started strong, he soon realized he couldn't keep this up. As his hands started to droop, he looked in horror as he watched the enemy begin to defeat his friends and family fighting down below. What was he to do? Suddenly, Moses felt a rock being placed under him and strong arms reaching out and lifting his arms up. You see, Moses hadn't come to that hill alone. His brother Aaron and his friend Hur had come along with him. When they saw his strength waning, they reached out and held up the hands of their friend. They stayed there until sunset and Israel defeated their enemy.

And so it is with teaching! We come into our classrooms with plans, energy, and enthusiasm. We know there will be battles, but we also know that with God's presence, we can overcome. But as time passes, we are inundated with emails, conferences, struggling students, angry parents, schedule changes, personal struggles... and we begin to weaken. We feel our arms weakening and that optimism we started with beginning to buckle. That's when we discover the beauty of this calling. We're not called to this hill alone. Alongside us are the other amazing teachers. They offer us a hug or an encouraging look. They come to our rooms and pray with us and for us. They offer advice and counsel because they've walked similar roads. They fight WITH us and help us find ways for that struggling student to see victory. They leave that kind note on our desk (sometimes with chocolate). They hold up our arms when we're too weak to continue the battle. There are lots of victories along the way, and we're able to rejoice together, too. We laugh and joke and encourage one another. We know that as we fight this battle together, through the power of God and the support of each other, we will be victorious.

One of the greatest blessings I've discovered in teaching is the coworkers who become friends – family, really – along the way. I know at any moment I can go to one of them, and they will be there for me. Teaching is not a self-contained event. We must have relationships with those around us. We must rely on others and be there for them when they need it. And after all, isn't this how the body of Christ is meant to function? I Corinthians 12:26 says, "If one part suffers, every part suffers with it; if one part is honored, every part rejoices with it." We must learn to listen to, rely on, pray for, and support each other. So, when the sun sets on our teaching career, we can look back and see God's hand at work and His love shown through those we're blessed to have holding up our hands.

LESSON LEARNED

We need each other. God designed us to be in supportive relationships for strength to complete the tasks He has set before us.

When Moses' hands grew tired, they took a stone and put it under him and he sat on it. Aaron and Hur held his hands up—one on one side, one on the other—so that his hands remained steady till sunset. Exodus 17: 12

Personal Reflection

_____

_____

_____

_____

_____

_____

_____

_____

_____

_____

_____

_____

_____

_____

_____

_____

CHAPTER 13

HANDWRITING WITH TEARS

S everal years into my stretch of teaching, Johnny entered my classroom and my heart. I do love all my students, but every once in a while, one comes along that pierces my heart and sinks in. It's almost like I see myself in those students. They remind me of my own struggles and inadequacies and I am inspired to help them.

Johnny had such a sweet and quirky innocence about him that I hadn't seen in a while. To others he was annoying, but to me he was enchanting. I loved his gangly walk, his messy hair, and his need to please. His past educational experiences had made him and his parents quite wary .. and weary. Since he had some catching up to do, he and I had to develop a good relationship quickly. We connected almost immediately.

Johnny needed extra time on tasks, the use of a multiplication chart to work facts, and help with organization. He struggled with cutting and gluing, keeping pencils sharp, finding his jacket, and remembering his lunch. However, nothing compared to his struggle to write in cursive.

At our school, students were expected to know how to write in cursive by the time they cross the threshold into my classroom. This immersion helps students practice their new skill. Most enjoy writing like a grown-up, but Johnny hated writing, whether it was manuscript or cursive. As was his nature, he spent way too much time bucking the system, which left very little time to actually work. The day finally came for the resisting to end.

While the rest of the class busily worked on projects, Johnny reluctantly stood at my desk. I pulled out a small table, laid out paper and placed a pencil in his hand. He stood as I worked and as I prayed. I would glance his way every few minutes but left him on his own. Eventually, I could feel the tension leave his hand. He relaxed and wrote. After writing a few shaky words, I turned and caught his eyes filled with tears. We smiled at each other and we knew. He knew he could do the work, and I knew Johnny had just made a huge break-through into accepting and following.

At unexpected times, usually in the middle of a challenging lesson, I remember Johnny. He worked so hard, and it lifted my heart. I learned the rewards of patience and persistence that year. I don't know who grew more, him or me, but I do know that God led, and we followed, and that made all the difference.

LESSON LEARNED
Patience and persistence pay off. Don't back down from challenges.
Let us not become weary in doing good, for at the proper time we will reap a harvest if we do not give up.
Galatians 6:9

Personal Reflection

_____
_____
_____
_____
_____
_____
_____
_____
_____
_____
_____
_____
_____
_____
_____
_____
_____
_____
_____
_____
_____
_____
_____
_____
_____
_____

CHAPTER 14
AMAZING GRACE

"Well, yes, she is!" I heard as I stepped into the town library with my summer reading books in hand. The librarian, a long-time friend, filled me in on the part of the conversation I had missed. A library patron who was standing where she could see out of the window, had commented, "Here comes a teacher-looking person," as I walked up to the library. Introductions were made as the three of us laughed at the coincidence.

A teacher-looking person. "What a compliment," I thought as I drove home. What does a teacher *look* like? What was there about me that said "teacher"? I was wearing a T-shirt, jean shorts, and sandals. This is not the first time someone has identified me as a teacher when I was not at school. While walking through the zoo with my grandson, I was listening to him read the plaques out loud in front of several exhibits. We were deep in conversation about predators versus prey when someone standing next to me asked, "Are you a teacher?" I said that I was and again thought how humbling to be defined as such.

My journey to become a certified teacher has been the culmination of many circumstances. I have had many "titles" in my life: daughter, sister, student, Christ-follower, wife, mother, pastor's wife, and grandmother. Each role is a mixture of blessing and responsibility, joy and pain. There have been circumstances that have altered some of those roles. Throughout the fabric of my life, though, one constant thread has been teaching. I didn't realize it, though, not until I came to Hope Elementary.

I had taught my children at home for 21 years and enjoyed seeing their moments of learning and grasping difficult concepts. However, there is a difference in teaching someone else's children in a classroom. While the academic curriculum and results are similar, the method is different.

How could I step into a classroom and be effective? Through mentoring, training, and experience, God showed a new plan and purpose for me. Each year in the classroom is better than the last. Each student is a joy, leaving a lasting print on my heart. Each class is exhausting, wonderful work. I began to rediscover a passion for teaching that had really been there all the time. It was WHO I was, not WHAT I was, all along. Teachers ARE; no degree or certificate can create a teacher. We teach because that is who God created us to be; we can do no other thing. We pour out of what God has given us; that outpouring gives us life in return.

It is still humbling to think that I have been included in this wonderful group known as teachers. No one is more amazed than I. To think that God's plan for me has brought such meaning and purpose to a life that was so broken----this is truly His amazing grace.

LESSON LEARNED

It's not over 'til it's over! He has a plan, a purpose and a place for each of us. His name is Faithful and True.

"For I know the plans I have for you," declares the LORD, "plans to prosper you and not to harm you, plans to give you hope and a future."
Jeremiah 29:11

Personal Reflection

_____
_____
_____
_____
_____
_____
_____
_____
_____
_____
_____
_____
_____
_____
_____
_____
_____
_____
_____
_____
_____

CHAPTER 15
LESSONS LEARNED

As summer is ending and the first day of school is just around the corner, I find myself reflecting. This is one of my favorite times of the year. I've been blessed to be able to minister to children for over thirty years in various roles: as a principal, teacher, instructional specialist, and ministry leader. The single most important role that I have held by far has been that of a parent. In each role, I've learned some valuable lessons throughout the years, but I believe that the most valuable lessons I've learned came through parenting my three children. My girls are now adults, but I still remember those last days of summer when they were young and we were getting ready for yet another school year! Days were spent in mad rush shopping for special school clothes and hunting feverishly for the perfect backpack. And don't forget the requisite reams of notebook paper, the pens and pencils that had to be just right, and the glue sticks and crayons! Those days are gone, but I now have the joy of watching my daughter and grandson prepare for the new school year. I help as only a grandmother can do, and share some of what I've learned with her as she, like her mother before her, learns the ropes of parenting and school days.

Some of the lessons I learned as a parent came easy; others I learned the hard way. I'd like to take this time to reflect and share with you some of the most important lessons I've learned over the years.

I learned early in my parenting years that the Scriptures are the ultimate authority when it comes to parenting. Whenever I would wish I had a training guide for parents, God would always remind me that He had already supplied guidance in His Word, which the Aposotle Paul states "is useful for teaching, rebuking, correcting and training in righteousness, so that the servant of God may be thoroughly equipped for every good work" (II Timothy 3: 16). The Word of God contains Biblical principles that can be applied to each and every aspect of life, including raising godly children. Are you trying to teach your child the importance of choosing good friends? I Corinthians 15:33 says, "Do not be misled; Bad company corrupts good character." Are you trying to instill a strong work ethic in your child? Proverbs 10:4 states, "Lazy hands make for poverty, but diligent hands bring wealth."

Teach and expect obedience from your child. You will not be able to train your child emotionally, cognitively, or spiritually if he does not obey you or others placed in authority over him. As a parent, it is your responsibility to set clear, consistent, and developmentally appropriate rules for your child in your home as well as for your child when he is away from home. A vital aspect to remember is that learning is often caught, not taught. This means that children tend to follow what they see more than what they hear. Simply stating and enforcing the rules is not enough; as parents we must model obedience to the Word of God and the authorities placed over us in front of our children. (Luke 6:40)

The goal of every parent is to raise responsible children. Far too often, well-meaning parents hinder their children from receiving natural consequences for inappropriate behavior. It's the teacher's fault the homework did not get turned in. It's the coach's fault that your child did not make the team. You want your child to be able to function successfully and become self-disciplined. A child can be taught responsibility as early as age three with simple tasks such as picking up his toys, helping mommy clean off the table after dinner, and straightening up his room before bed. By the age of eight, your child should be able to set his own alarm clock, get himself up, get dressed, and be ready for school on time. (Proverbs 22:6)

Enjoy your children. "Children are a heritage from the Lord." (Psalm 127:3) I know there may be times your child doesn't feel like a gift – the colicky nights, the trips to the doctor, or the discipline we often must employ as our children grow and mature, all on top of the busy and exhausting pace of life. Often it may seem that it takes all of your energy to simply feed and bathe your child and then tuck him into bed after a long day at work. It can be a challenge to set aside time from your busy schedule to spend time with your children, yet I urge you to do it. Second only to God and your spouse, the relationship with your children is the most important relationship you will have on this Earth. You were intended to disciple and grow them into responsible Kingdom citizens. Building relationships involves spending time together. Spend time each day just talking with your child. This is not time to lecture but to sincerely ask about their day and share some things about your day if appropriate. Plan Family Nights and then schedule them on your calendar as you would any appointment. I remember Family Night at our house was every Friday night. We would play board games, watch movies, go bowling, or have devotion as a family. It was during those times we grew the most as a family unit.

Remember, your role as a parent is a serious call from God and His gift to you. You only have a short window of time to prepare your child to be a responsible Christian citizen who will make a difference in a secular world. It can be a daunting task, but God has provided everything we need as parents to raise godly children. Pray, study the Word of God, and build relationships with each other and with other Christian parents who will hold you accountable. You are training and discipling the future generation of Kingdom builders. (Luke 6:40)

LESSON LEARNED
The most important ministry for a parent is the discipleship of their own children.
Impress them on your children. Talk about them when you sit at home and when you walk along the road, when you lie down and when you get up.
Deuteronomy 6:7

PERSONAL REFLECTION

_____

_____

_____

_____

_____

_____

_____

CLOSING COMMENTS

You have had a glimpse into the classrooms of 10 educators. So, what is the major lesson that they learned? What was their primary take-a-way?

Through 211 years of teaching, we came to the realization that teaching is not just about "reading, writing, and arithmetic". While high test scores and producing productive citizens are good objectives, those are not our ultimate goals.

We believe education should be intentional, with the goal of inspiring and equipping the next generation to further God's Kingdom by cultivating a relationship with Christ. Our commitment to education is founded on the belief that children are a gift from God. As a result, we are committed to creating a learning environment where each child is viewed as a unique individual who needs a caring and stimulating environment to grow and mature spiritually, intellectually, emotionally, physically, and socially. Education involves more than a child's intellectual abilities, it should ultimately inspire learners to fulfill God's purpose in their lives.

ABOUT THE AUTHORS

Dr. Shailendra Thomas

Dr. Shailendra Thomas has served in Christian ministry for three decades, as women's and children's ministry leader, Bible study teacher, and seminar speaker. Dr. Thomas' experience in education extends over 30 years, serving as an elementary school teacher, instructional specialist, educational consultant, adjunct college professor, Sr. Administrator/Principal at Fellowship Christian Academy, Head of School at Scofield Christian School and National Accreditation Commissioner for the Association of Christian Schools International.

Dr. Thomas has recently been called to start a school in an underserved area of Dallas; however, her primary ministry is to her husband of 37 years, Richard, her three grown daughters, Lorren, Hillary, and Chelsea, and one grandson, Landon Blake. She enjoys reading, traveling, and entertaining during her spare time. Dr. Thomas has also co-authored two other books, *Coveted Conversations* and *Image Bearer*.

Becky Craig

Becky Craig has just finished her 30th year of teaching. She believes that learning can and should be fun and hands-on. One of her favorite things is to hear her students laugh and see them smile. She believes strongly in building relationships not only with her students, but with parents. Her classroom motto is Daniel 12:3, which talks about shinning like stars for Jesus in our words and our actions.

She has been married to her husband, John, for 38 years. They have four adult children. She also has two sons-in-law, four grandchildren, and a dog. She enjoys spending time with her family which is spread out across the country and even overseas. She is an avid reader, loves to travel, and enjoys the gift of hospitality. She is working on becoming a strong prayer warrior and an encourager to others.

Laurie Thames

This is Laurie Thames' 29th year of teaching. She taught first grade and has now been in kindergarten for the last 21 years. As a teacher she loves being one of the first "stamps in wet cement" on a child's life as they move into the area of academic learning. She believes each child is a gift from God and enjoys developing in them their relationship with God, believing they will become great lights in a dark world.

She has been married to her husband Jim for 31 years. They have two daughters who are now married and pursuing careers in counseling and medicine. Some of her favorite things to do outside the classroom are to spend time with family and friends. She loves sharing her home with others along with reading, gardening, and quiet times on her patio.

Trisha Baker

Trisha Baker is in her 15th year of teaching and has taught in both public and Christian schools. She believes that teaching is all about relationships with students, parents, and colleagues. She loves to have her students fully engaged in their learning and use all areas of her classroom whether they are in their reading nook or up on their feet at the whiteboards. Math is the subject she especially loves to teach and get students excited about, but she wants her students enjoying all aspects of their education. Every year she comes up with a new theme for her classroom after praying about it and asking the Lord for His direction and emphasis for the year. Over the years her students have enjoyed themes based on the Monopoly board game, The Price Is Right game show, and an escape room. Each theme has a built-in spiritual component and incorporates a Bible verse or passage.

Trisha has two children who are enjoying the benefits of Christian school education and have even survived having her as a teacher. She enjoys spending time with her family, church activities, shopping, and taking mission trips.

Corrienne Mullins

Corrienne Mullins is in her 19th year of teaching. She felt the call to teach even as a young child and can remember many afternoons making her brother play school. She loves teaching and is thankful that God called her into the ministry of discipling young minds. She believes teaching is a high calling to inspire students' love of God and learning. When a student makes a connection or has that "lightbulb moment," it makes the work worth it.

Corrienne has been married to her husband, Matt, for 4 years. They are currently in the adoption process and are excited to see how God is going to grow their family. She enjoys spending time with friends and serving in her church. She also likes to try her hand at DIY projects and crafting. She views life as a lot of everyday adventures. Her prayer is that God will use her to love and be a blessing to others in her life.

Dianna Hatfield

Dianna Hatfield has been teaching for 15 years in both public and private schools in North Texas. She has followed this calling since graduating from East Texas Baptist University with a BSE in Elementary Education and Music. After teaching music for two years, she felt led to teach in a contained classroom and has been there ever since where she has taught 5th grade and 3rd grade. She loves to see the transition from lower elementary when students begin to read to learn.

Dianna is married to Joel Hatfield, a senior consultant and a vicar in the Episcopal Church. They met and married in Kansas City, MO in 1990 and have a daughter, Hannah Rose who is eighteen. Hannah attends Dallas Baptist University and plans to graduate with a Music Education degree in 2020.

Dianna enjoys spending time with friends and family and is involved in church ministries. When time is available, she loves to scrapbook and decorate her home.

Rhiannon Thurman

Rhiannon Thurman has taught preschool for 11 years at various Christian schools. Her favorite thing to do is to read aloud to her students. She enjoys making stories come alive by making them fun and interactive. Her goal is to infuse the joy of learning into the classroom by introducing engaging hands-on learning activities. She is passionate about helping young children discover the immense love God has for them. Galatians 6:9 is her favorite Bible verse, and she finds comfort and encouragement in knowing that the Lord will reward hard work done in His name if we do not give up.

She recently celebrated her fourteenth year of marriage to her husband Eric and they have three daughters and one son-in-law. They also have two cats - one is abnormally large!

She believes Audrey Hepburn said it best when she said: "As you grow older, you will discover that you have two hands, one for helping yourself, the other for helping others." She is grateful for the many blessings the Lord has given her and her family. She is currently learning to share these blessings with refugees in Dallas.

Sara Malone

Sara Malone is in her 20th year of teaching. She loves being in the classroom and wants her students to grow both academically and spiritually. Her goal is to help develop a strong spiritual foundation in their lives, one on which they can build all future learning. She enjoys seeing the "aha" moment on a student's face when a concept is understood.

Sara graduated from Philadelphia College of Bible with

degrees in both Bible and Education. Her teaching experiences have been in public, private, and home schools. Sara has been married to her husband, George, for 34 years and together they have 2 adult daughters. In her free time she enjoys camping and hiking, especially with family and friends.

Shayne Kasselman

Shayne Kasselman, originally from South Louisiana, currently resides in a suburb of Dallas. She is the mother of four children and "Mimi" to her three grandchildren. Ms. Kasselman homeschooled for twenty-one years before entering the classroom at a private Christian school to share her love of teaching with other children. She is a member of Sunnyvale Town Council and co-chairs the Library Board. She continues to share her love for her Lord, for learning, and for books with her first grade class and her grandchildren.

Rachel Montgomery

Rachel Montgomery has been teaching for 15 years in grade levels ranging from preschool through high school. She is grateful for her daily interactions with her students and enjoys collaborating with them as they make connections between their curriculum and Biblical principles.

Rachel has been married to her husband for 26 wonderful years and from this union God blessed them with two adult sons and one teenage daughter. Rachel loves reading, exercising with her family, playing with her two puppies, and rooting for the Boston Red Sox.

www.ingramcontent.com/pod-product-compliance
Lightning Source LLC
LaVergne TN
LVHW041234080426
835508LV00011B/1208